Haiku
and Other Poems

Kalyan Chaudhury

INDIA • SINGAPORE • MALAYSIA

ISBN 979-8-89415-236-3

Table of Contents

1. Haiku...7

2. An unknown Woman...59

3. An unknown Woman–2....................................61

4. A COUPLE 62

5. A Letter 64

6. A ROBBER AND A THIEF................................65

7. A tale of a STONE 66

8. APRIL! APRIL! 67

9. BOGTUI: 21.3.2022 69

10. To the citizens of Troy....................................71

11. The Crocodile and the Vagina........................73

12. Democracy????????.......................................74

13. Development 76

14. Endless 77

15. In memory of POTTAM HUNGI......................78

16. Last Day of the Spring 79

17. Love...81

18. My Poem..82

19. Nobody knows 84

20. PHOENIX 85

21. Please wait 86

22. In the Rainy Evening...................................87

23. Shut up 88

24. Silence 89

25. A dialogue: Spring and Monsoon 90

26. The Autumn 92

27. The Birds...93

28. The Circus..94

29. The Dogs 96

30. The Jungle - Lore 97

31. To the Poets and Artists................................99

32. The Sword of Democles................................ 100

33. The Weather Cock.. 101

34. To MIRAJ, my friend 102

35. To My Children.. 104

36. To the Killers... 106

37. To us.. 108

38. My last love... 109

39. My last love: 2... 110

40. Nursery Rhyme 111

                                    Table of Contents

41. Nursery Rhyme: 2 113

42. Nursery Rhyme: 3 115

43. Nursery Rhyme: 4 117

44. To my Love 119

45. To my Love: 2 120

46. To you 121

47. To You 122

48. English version of a Urdu poem
    "Fark sirf itna sa tha"... 123

49. Who am I?... 125

50. Who are they? 126

51. Why 127

52. With an apology to GOLDING
    (the Nobel Laureate) 128

53. Yesterday, Today, Tomorrow............................... 129

54. A Farce???.. 130

55. An imaginary conversation 131

56. An Ode to the People 132

57. Fall of Macbeth 134

58. Govt. Sign-Board but..... 136

59. HOMO Sapiens... 137

60. HUNGER and FOOD 139

61. I Can.. 141

62. If you...142

63. Last love: 3 143

64. Love...144

65. Man is Mortal..146

66. New Nursery Rhyme: 1..............................147

67. New Nursery Rhyme: 2..............................148

68. New Nursery Rhyme: 3..............................149

69. New Nursery Rhyme: 4..............................150

70. New Nursery Rhyme: 5..............................151

71. New Nursery Rhyme: 6..............................152

72. New Nursery Rhyme: 7..............................153

73. One day in the Book Fair 154

74. Prayer of Winter 155

75. Problems and Solutions.............................156

76. Tell Me 157

77. The Boy and His Mother (land) 158

78. The Handkerchief......................................159

79. The Kiss 160

80. To the PIG-STY Goers................................161

81. To the Capitalism 162

Haiku

1. The cat is roaring
   Like a lion
   While drinking milk

2. She is shouting
   At others
   Having stolen
   Treasure

3. The swine
   Wears
   A pearl necklace

4. The monk laughs
   In the kitchen
   Cooking gas

5. The monk
   Speaks to us
   Wait for good days

6.   Humpty Dumpty
Sat on a wall
Humpty Dumpty
Had a great fall
But now Aunty
Is on the wall

7.   Little Miss Muffet
Sat on a tuffet
Making the spider's net

8.   The girl eats gold
The boy doesn't know
There is a hut yonder

9.   The wind is blowing
With sweet smell
I look at your
Photograph

10.   The breeze
Is behind the curtain
Call her

11.   It was C.U.
       I was in the class
       You were not there

12.   It was College Square
       The answer was in the air
       Blue water called us

13.   Two bags talk
       Two bags walk
       In the park

14.   I waited
       On the platform
       A flying bird whistled
       You were coming

15.   A frog jumped
       To the evening star
       And became a Prince

16.   The train was running
       You put your head
       On my shoulder
       It was a soothing Noon

17.   A pregnant time
       Calls
       The Spring Thunder
       Roars
       The Beauty sleeps

18.   It was evening
       The storm touched
       The Queen
       And vanished in the Blue

19.   Pottam, the girl
       Daughter of the soil
       Was killed
       By carpet bombing

20.   The land was theirs
       The hills were theirs
       Still Bloody Bustards
       Looted them

21.   Do you know
       All my words
       Are for you?

22.   Scorching heat
        Of the sun
        Always says to me
        "Rain Will come"

23.   Who is the foreigner?
        Who never sleeps?
        Who is becoming
        A piece of stone?

24.   Who wakes early
        In the morning
        To blow away
        The candle light?

25 .   You don't know
        Juliet is in the balcony
        Only knows
        The falling Sparrow

26.   Encounter
        Three bullets
        Democracy

27.   An apple
A knife
Are on the plate
They have fallen in Love

28.   A piece of Juliet's heart
Cried out
"Come Night, come Romeo"

29.   She is coming
With Light
But I am blind

30.   Ru said to Mircha
"I have told my mother
That you have kissed
On my forehead"

31.   I know
You have come out
To see me

32.   When you
Hold my hand
I sing

                                    Haiku and Other Poems

33.   It is Dawn
        It is Noon
        It is Evening
        Always a leaf
        Is falling down

34.   The trees
        Give shadow
        Waiting for
        Death Sentence

35.   Flowers fall
        Flowers fall
        But blossoming
        Garden is there

36.   Hans Christian Anderson Museum
        Norway
        On a rack a portrait of a princess
        Written below
        Hans loved her

37.   Without you
Plains become hilly
How will I cross
A real mountain?

38.   Your house is
Covered by curtains
A wayfarer wind am I
Calling you always

39.   A drop of water
Saves a dying bird
A drop of Tear
Falls on the little bud

40.   Cows and Monkeys
Are our gods
Nobody can save us
From disaster

41.   Who are you reader
Hindu or Muslim?
Then no need
To read my poem

Only you can read
When you are Homo Sapiens

42.   When will you
        Go to Sea?
        Bring a handful of sands
        For me

43.   Happiness is
        Allegorical
        But unhappiness
        Is real

44.   It is dark
        Fireflies in bushes
        Write a book
        On happiness

45.   My Love don't go
        With that boy
        Don't talk to him
        I am jealous

46.   When I looked
At you
A river of light
Was flowing

47.   It is very hot today
Do you have a
Canopy tree?

48.   We are getting old
But young within
We live in memories

49.   How are the river
And the boatman?
Still they are loving
Each other?

50.   There is no love
There is a habit
A dog is shouting outside

51.   Can you hear me?
The street lights
The footpath

The cars
And the buses are blushing

52.   When I go to you
        For Alms
        You give me a balm
        For my bruised heart

53.   When we were playing
        I knew not
        Who you were

54.   In happiness
        I saw you
        I found you
        In sorrow

55.   When I lost you
        I hid you
        Untamed life was flowing

57.   LOVE is so short
        Forgetting is so long

56.   I saw the Volga
        And the Ganges In your eyes

58.   40 dead bodies
        The King was
        Enthroned

59.   Together we ate
        Together we walked
        And we separated

60.   The eyes were
        Dark and deep
        Like a lake
        I longed to take bath
        Long long ago

61.   I have got a Time Machine
        Everything is happening
        Before me
        Like a Swan
        You're coming down

        Who decorates you?

Thomas Mann
In his Black Swan!

62.   Historical
        Dubbledecker
        Is taking us
        To the unknown land

63.   That is not a train
        A white horse
        Last ride together
        Browning I remember

64.   Now we are
        In wonderland
        Black road goes
        To the king's palace

65.   We are inside the palace
        You are smart enough
        To fix me on the floor
        You're marvellous

66.   From a dream
       To a reality
       You're eager to go
       But I have fallen
       From the horse

67.   You're unique
       On the earth
       Never you will
       Take birth

68.   Invincible you are
       Always like adventure

69.   The system can
       Never digest you
       Unpredictable

       Understands a very few

70.   So fortunate I am
       Having seen you
       It is a spectacular view

71.   Tell her today
        I am ashamed within
        I could not catch
        The running Green

72.   O sun O moon
        Do you know her?
        In the flower of life
        She is the nectar

73.   Earning money
        Is a fun
        What are you?
        I am a politician

74.   Rabindranath
        You should be living
        At this hour
        India is a
        Fen of stagnant water!

75.   Spine is for sale
        Spline is for sale
        Announces the RASCAL!

76.   I am hungry
Give me some RELIGION
I will eat!

77.   I am a HINDU
I am ill
Badly I need BLOOD
Give me only HINDU BLOOD!

78.   I am also ill
MUSLIM I am
Give me only
MUSLIM BLOOD!

79.   Old love
Never rusts
Irrespective of
Creed and caste

80.   The deer
And the hunter
Never think alike

81.   Enemies
        Of the people
        Become the TEACHERS

82.   In the Darkness
        Be the sun
        Yourself

83.   A roasted bird
        Comes before you
        There comes the Vote!

84.   War will end
        The children will play
        In joy
        The old tree is waiting

85.   Have you
        Ever been lost
        In a jungle
        Where never
        Reaches the sun?

86.   In the mountain
       Of sorrow
       There is a hope of a Stone!

87.   Burn
       The old dry leaves
       And find your way

88.   It is true
       His body is burning
       After death
       But before death
       His Mind has burnt

89.   My home
       Was on fire
       You put out it
       With your tears!

90.   Everybody talks
       ABOUT JOHN HENRY
       Nobody about you
       MARY
       Mary Magdalene!

91.   Two babies
       Are sucking
       Their mother's breast
       And they are fighting as well!

92.   What is FACT?
       What is REALITY?
       What is TRUTH?

93.   Memories
       Are knocking
       At the DOOR

       Please come in!

94.   Few monsters
       No fear
       My dear

95.   You have Wings
       Why are you
       Crawling?

96. Insult
     Is in MIND
     But plastic
     In DUSTBIN

97. STORM
     Can kill a TREE
     Not the GRASS

98. "Have Patience"
     The rain says
     To the SEED

99. You
     Are killing BEES
     No TOMORROW
     Will come

100. Respect
     PEOPLE
     But
     Not the STATE!!

　　　　　　　　　Haiku and Other Poems

101.   What we are carrying
        Is not our Pain
        But what we are hiding!

102.   NETAJI said
        Give me blood
        I will give you FREEDOM
        But today
        The politician says
        Give me VOTE
        I will suck your BLOOD!!

103.   What I eat
        What I drink
        You have given me
        My MOTHERLAND!!

104.   I am standing
        In front of my OLD HOUSE
        My Childhood is playing THERE!

105 .   The CLOWN
        Is on the THRONE
        The Palace
        Becomes a CIRCUS!!

106.   The teacher of the animals
Is taking attendance
All are present
Except Chameleons and Donkeys
Chameleons are giving lectures
And Donkeys are the listeners!!

107.   Dethrone the King
Dethrone the Queen
The little CHILDREN are crying!

108 .   He steals Rs100
And is a THIEF
But the person
Who has taken
A loan of THOUSAND CRORES
From a BANK
And will never repay
He is CORPORATE!!

109.   Similar
Are Hand made Bread
And the GOVERNMENT!
If you don't turn
The Bread over

It will burn
If you don't turn
The Government over
The PEOPLE will burn!!

110.   I have seen
Many HUMAN BEIINGS
Without any DRESS
I have seen
Many DRESSES
Without HUMAN BEINGS
INSIDE!!

111.   Do you have
Any IDEOLOGY?
Yes,I have
Are you MARXIST?
No Sir
Are you NATIONALIST?
No Sir
Then
What are you?
I am CORRUPTIONIST!!

112.   We have not seen
        Each other for a long time
        We say
        To ourselves
        We will meet again
        Or
        We will never meet again!!

113.   To whom it may concern
        Declare THEFT as a PROFESSION!!!

114 .   Don't drink WINE
        Drink POWER!!

115.   I am thirsty
        But WATER
        Is everywhere!!

116 .   Don't be MAD
        Use the FIRE!!

117.   The darker
        Is the NIGHT
        The nearer
        Is the DAWN!!

118 .   "Where is your clothing, o King?"
The Child says
"I am naked
So what?"
Answers the shameless KING!!

119.   Throughout my life
I have been writing
An unfinished POEM!!

120.   The tree of pain
Will bear a sweet fruit
Someday!!

121.   People
Stand in queue
For selecting the persons
Who will TORTURE them
For the next FIVE YEARS!!

122.   With an apology
To Robert Browning
Last ride together in a RICKSHAW
After the ride you vanished
In the BIUE!!

123.   Beware
TORTURERS
LAXMI BAI of JHANSI
Is sharpening the SWORD!!

124.   Where the mind
Is without fear
Come back the FREEDOM FIGHTERS!!

125 .   DEAD BODIES
Are very happy
Burst into LAUGHTER
To welcome the new
OPPRESSOR!!

126.   POWER
And CAPITAL
Kiss
Each other!!

127.   Villagers fight
Villagers die
Politicians
Play CHESS!!

128. Poets and Artists
Are in search of
The SPINES
In darkness!!

129. BLACk is BLACK
WHITE is WHITE
But different shades are there
You can't them HIDE!!

130. Sword of Democles
Under which
You SLEEP!!

131. Teacher: Which PROFESSION
Do you want to try?
Student: I want to be
A member of the PIGSTY!!

132. Mirror: Why are you cleaning me?
Aunty:Because I am looking dirty!
Mirror: Then clean YOURSELF not ME!!

133.   PAIN
Has no weight
But it is
Very PAINFUL
To bear IT!!

134.   CAPITALISM
Will reign for EVER
Good days come NEVER
If you wait for
GOD'S FAVOUR!!!

135.   What is the 8th WONDER
On the EARTH?
SPINELESS
HOMO SAPIENS
Take BIRTH!!

136.   ADIEU DEMOCRACY
16 lives you have snatched
Within few days
Still you are athirst for BLOOD
No longer flowers will be flowers
Readily they will be VOLCANOES!!

137.   What is a WAR - ZONE?
In EUROPE
Russia and Eukrane
In BEGALI VERSION
It is PANCHAET ELECTION!!

138.   Last day
From Hills to Bay
In some places
ELECTION
Peacefully was DONE
In other places
No DEATH COULD
Disturb the COMMISSION!!

139.   Those who became STONE
And EDUCATED to the BACK BONE
Could not hear the SCREAM of SILENCE
Even could not write a SENTENCE
Only PEACEFUL TERRORISM reigns!!!

140.   They want badly
To SERVE us
That is why
They are fighting

And killing each other
How KIND they are!!!

141. The CHAMELEON
Committed suicide
Because it could not defeat
The politicians and artists
In CHANGING COLOURS
NOW and THEN
No LOSS only GAIN!!

142. The PIGSTY going CRIMINALS
NEVER care for ANYTHING!
Only 55 lives forever GONE
With the WIND!
Only PEACEFUL TERRORISM reigns!!!

143. With your eyes
You can see
Many other things
But you need
A mirror
To see your face!!

144.   We know
        The King
        Is naked
        Etc etc.
        But
        Who will write
        The POEM
        Where a CHILD says
        "O POET
        Where is your CLOTHING??"

145.   A dying Soldier
        Cries out.
        Whose name?
        His Country's name?
        The ruler's name?
        Or
        Only
        His MOTHER'S NAME??

146.   Tell me where
        Dolls
        Are well dressed
        But
        Women

Are moving NAKED
After being RAPED!!!

147.   The Rhinoceros
Was too proud
To have the thickest skin
But
Today he has felt ashamed
To learn
"A politician's SKIN
Is THICKER than his!!!"

148 .   That day
I told you few words
But
Those were carried away
By the mystic wind
You could not hear me!!

149.   A butterfly
Sat on a bomb
Hidden in a flower
She was safe
After some time
She sat on a sentence

Of a Leader
She was torn into pieces
In a moment!!!

150 .   Once dreams
        Said to LIFE
        "When will we be TRUE?"
        LIFE replied
        "NEVER
        If you become TRUE
        I will be VALUELESS!!!"

151.   She is
        At your door
        She is HUNGRY
        Give her FOOD
        She is NAKED
        Give her CLOTHING
        She has no HOME
        Give her SHELTER
        She is beautiful
        Love her
        She is your MOTHERLAND!!!

152 .   You
         Have been throwing stones
         To me
         For a pretty long time
         I have never taken
         REVENGE
         I have built a HOUSE
         With your stones
         Please throw more STONES
         I love you!!!

153 .   Last Night
         The child got
         A White plate
         Full of white flowers
         In his dream!!

154.   You are not you
         Eyes are not dancing
         Eyebrows are not calling
         You are no longer you
         I don't know WHY!!!

155 .   I knew a STAR
        He couldn't even speak
        So long he lived
        After his death
        He has spoken
        For EIGHT minutes!!!

156 .   We live in Memories
        Memories live in LOVE
        Love lives in
        Enchanted Fire
        Enchanted Fire
        Lives in YOUR EYES!!!

157.   A mountain of words
        You gave me in my bag
        This was my Happiness
        But wrongly she called it her Sorrow!!!

158.   The hungry gardener
        Is protecting the flowers
        Of the garden!!!

159.   When you love me
        Love like the Facebook
        Where anybody can be restricted
        At any time!!!

160.   Who are you reader
        Doesn't want to know your past?
        Who are you reader
        Always wants to know my caste?
        Who are you reader
        Wants to know my gender?
        Who are you reader
        Always a contender!!!

161.   When I will be in London
        Please don't phone me
        Write a letter to me
        I keep it in my pocket
        Wherever I will be!!!

162.   Do you love me
        My Love?
        You have not heard
        Calls of a dove
        At a lonely noon

                          Haiku and Other Poems

You have not seen
A Butterfly
On a railway track
After a few seconds
It will be run over!!!

163.   It comes to my mind
That I loved you
The whistle of a train
Carried you
To a distant land
It comes to my mind
Many deaths I crossed
My name was crushed
Under the wheels of time!!!

164.   Don't talk of food
Don't talk of land
Don't talk of sand
Don't talk you Dude
About the band
Of robbers and
The thieves' plan
Only drink wine
And say, "Fine, fine!"

165.   Bidding is on
        A hurricane, a tyfoon
        It's a boon
        It's a boon
        The butterfly is in the Cocoon!!!

166.   The circus is shown
        My eyes, my mouth,my bone
        My circle, my square,my cone
        My enzyme,my hormone
        But paddy is not sown!!!

167.   Players are not playing
        The referee is blowing
        Whistle and throwing
        Balls and kicking
        He is left in and left out
        He is grass as well as cow
        He can stand erect and bow
        Only a black cat says, "Miaow, Miaow!!!"

169.   Where is the pond?
        No pond Sir
        Where are the Rivers?
        Only two are there

                          Haiku and Other Poems

One is Akash Ganga
Another in my eyes!!!

170.   As we grow old
We fall in love
With SILENCE!!!

171.   "There wil be
No hungry children
They can drink liquid
Moonlight easily"

172.   "No need to eat anything
Only eat cowdung cake
No need to drink water
Only drink cow urine"..........
An old jungle proverb

173.   "Honourable owner
Please make me a tree
I'll give you shadow
And fresh air
Even when you are going
To kill me"..........
An old village proverb

Kalyan Chaudhury

174.   We, middle class blues
Live in luxury
But talk of the downtrodden!!!

175.   Get your experience
Burnt and beaten
As the steel was tempered!!!

176.   You may pluck the flowers
But can't restrict
The Spring Thunder!!!

177.   I know you'll never call me
Still I am standing
Before Your HOUSE!!

178.   What is love?
When you are in trans
A face is in the mist ....

179.   Each of us says
"Revolution"
But all are like lonely Islands!!!

180.   My last song is waiting
        For your golden touch!!!

181.   My love have pity on me
        My eyes have lost light
        Give me some of yours!!!

182.   A Poor man took loan
        From a Bank
        He couldn't repay
        His house was sold
        In a Rich man's case
        He ran away
        And the Bank was bankrupt!!!

183.   If you are not STUPID
        Who will listen to my lecture?
        If you are not POOR
        Whom will I give dole?

184.   He had been a beggar
        He was a guard
        Now he is the SON of GOD!!!

185.   We are not DEAD
We are LIVING
This is DEVELOPEMENT!!!

186.   You loved me
To forget your SORROW
But I loved you at first sight!!!

187.   Today I love you
Also you love me
What will happen tomorrow?

188.   A school truant CLOUD
Takes classes
Of the mystic WIND!!!

189.   Give me water of LOVE
I'll drink it to the Lees!!!

190.   I wanted to sleep on the FLOOR
You said, "Let me clean it!!!"

191.   You plucked the flower
        A thorn pricked the ring finger
        Again the needle pricked the same
        Still why did you make the garland
        In the moonlit night???

192.   Walls have ears
        But the mountains don't
        Now tell me
        "Why did you marry me?"

193.   ___Where are you going?
        ___I am going to the Pigsty
        ___What will you do there?
        ___I'll make Constitutional Cowdung Cakes!!

194.   My love, my old flame, my Poet
        You came to me
        After a long time
        I was eager to listen to a Poem
        But you wanted Rs 100 from Me!!!

194.   Neither a Hindu is in danger
       Nor a Muslim
       Our money in bank is in danger
       Public sector is in danger
       Real price of harvest is in danger
       To divert our attention
       Who is playing mischief?

195.   Truth wishes
       To express itself
       Lie wishes
       To suppress itself!!!

196.   ..... Please quarrel with me
       ..... Why?
       ..... I'll feel no pain when you go away!!!!

197.   I can lift a large Stone
       But I can't lift the weight
       Of your "No!!!"

198.   I can face a sharp Sword
       But I can't face your Anger!!!

199.   A forest fire couldn't
        Melt me
        But your "Yes" melted me!!!

200.   LAWS rule the POOR
        The RICH rules LAWS!!!

201.   The King --- I am looking dirty
        The Queen --- I am also
        The Minister --- Please don't worry.
        I'll clean the mirror.
        The King and the Queen --- Still we are looking
        dirty
        The Jester --- Better clean YOURSELVES not
        the MIRROR!!!

202.   Crow --- Why are you in the cage?
        Parrot --- Because I can speak!!!

203.   ---Who are you?
        ---I am a politician
        ---What are you?
        ---I have been looting people from time
        immemorial!!!

204.   Exploit people in such a way ....
They have to think
Development means
"They are not DEAD!!!"

205.   ..... Sir/Madam, a thief is caught
..... Make him/her the leader!

206.   The more you are in CORRUPTION
The more you practise RELIGION!!!

207.   Take care of MINUTES
HOURS will take care of themselves!!!

208.   King ..... Vote is coming
Queen....But we need uneducated, weak, naked,
hungry, poor and slave people!!!

209.   Now you are drunk
You've lost COMMON SENSE
Give up wine of RELIGION!!!

210.   They offered the GIRL a role in a movie
        The GIRL accompanied them
        And SHE was gang-raped in a running cab
        Deaf and dumb TIME is passing by!!!

211.   Members of a PARTY
        Are CORRUPTED
        But the PARTY is CORRUPTION
        Free!!

212.   D. A. is OPTIONAL
        But "Theft" is COMPULSORY!!!

213.   The robber poses like a MONK
        The thief like a NUN
        A lot of money
        And a lot of fun!!!

214.   You are addicted to RELIGION
        But you are hungry and unemployed
        Your children are uneducated!!!

215.   All love stories are fairy tales
        What will happen to OURS???

216.   You threw stones at me
With those I've built my house
Thank you!!!

217.   Drink scripture
Eat scripture
All problems will be solved!!!

218.   My child is very hungry
Please give him some RELIGION!!!

219.   Unemployment is guaranteed
Poverty is ----
Not life but death is ----
Only say "Jai Shri Ram!!!"

220.   Love me like Facebook
At any moment you can restrict
me!!!

221.   ...... How many voices are there? Name them.
.... Two.
Active and passive.
...... Other voices?
.... Quasi passive and Cuckoo's voice!!!

222.   ..... Is Rice guaranteed?

..... No

..... Is Wheat guaranteed?

..... No

..... Is Clothing guaranteed?

..... No

..... Is Shelter guaranteed?

..... No

..... Then which is Guaranteed?

..... RAMbabu is Guaranteed!!!!

223.   ..... Sir, have you seen the
Hunger Index?

..... Yes

..... Is it wise to make the doors with 100 kg of
gold?

..... Why not? It is not my house but it's
Rambabu's!!!

224.   ..... Sir, theory of Darwin?

..... Cancelled

..... Mendeleev's periodic table?

..... Cancelled

..... Grant to the Science Congress?

..... Cancelled

..... Then?

..... Only Rum! Only Rum!!!

225.   He isn't afraid of War

Because the soldiers'll fight

He is afraid of Press-conference

Because he himself has to answer

The Questions!!!

226.   Behind the temple

No religion

No Rum

Only Election!!!

227.   "RUM" goes to your stomach

And makes you drunk

It goes to your brain

And makes you a fanatic

It is a god to an ignorant

It is a tool to a leader

To capture Voters!!!

228.   P M to the god
C M to the god
Our children are on the
FOOTPATH!!!

229.   Don't be afraid of WINTER
I've kept SPRING in my bag
Come and open it!

230.   A lover is like a child
Both feel pain
But can't tell anyone
About the same!!!

231.   Last night it rained
The soil lost her VIRGINITY!!!

232.   The more you are becoming blind
The keener your observation is
The more you are becoming deaf
The better you can listen
The more broken your leg is
The faster you can run!!!

233.   Worms inside destroy
       The chair
       Worms on it destroy
       The state!!!

234.   "Fingers refuse to write
       Eyes refuse to see
       Lips refuse to kiss"
       Says the dying TREE!!!

235.   I'm a fool
       I've sold my soul
       In lieu of little happiness!!!

236.   In youth he made tea
       By burning stove
       In middle age .....
       By burning Gujarat
       In old age .....
       By burning India!!!

An unknown Woman

At the age of eleven
She was married
A new place
A new man
A new family in Benaras

A year after her husband died
She never knew what a husband was

She came back to her mother
A widow was she
She fell on the thorns of Life
And was bleeding

A beautiful girl was she
Her long hair was cut
She cried bitterly
Wearing a White Sari

A Living Doll
In an area of Darkness
In her own family

Everyone used to curse her
Only her elder brother
Gave her some books
Her weapons
Her Future

A white statue worked
From morning to dusk
When it was midnight
She started reading

His elder brother failed
To arrange her remarriage
Everyone was against
WIDOW MARRIAGE

Bengal divided
Came the Black Day
Her family was settled
In Calcutta
She did not give up

An unknown Woman–2

She looked after
Her brother's children
When she got time
She read loudly
My mother, my Granny
Listened
I was also a listener

From my very boyhood
She had become my teacher
Many books, many stories
Many poems, many essays
Captivated me with awe

And I started writing
Inspired by my learned Aunt!

A COUPLE

A couple has come
To my house
It has many rooms
But there is no mouse

The couple says
"Does Honour live here?"
"No, he has left"
Is my answer

"Liar lives here
With dishonour
Only reigns Fear
With thief and robber"

"But we come here
In search of Honesty
Our teacher"

"He is gone
With his modesty"

"But Truth, our
Only son!"

"He has undergone
brain operation
But who are you Mr and Mrs?"

"We are LIFE and PEACE
Forever we are leaving
In DENMARK rotten is something!!"

A Letter

A letter was flying in the air
I called her Ophelia
I shouted, "Stop here"
She said, "I am Cloudia
Now I am becoming a leaf
Lost within a green tree"
"No problem I'll get you
You may be costly or free"
"STUPIDITY is in your backbone
How can you get?
We are thousands
"Don't try to overestimate"
Saying this she became a FAIRY QUEEN
And showed me a long magic wand
I cried out, "No need of that"
"Let me kiss on your left hand!!!"

A ROBBER AND A THIEF

I know a robber
I know a thief
Both are bosom friends
The robber poses
Like a MONK
The thief
Like a NUN
He sells the VILLAGE
To another robber
Who comes to the NUN
And marries her
Secretly
The MONK
AND the NUN
A lot of FUN
With money and gun!

A tale of a STONE

It is better
To look at the Beauty
From a distance

If you
Observe her closely
Some black spots
Are there

I have gone
To many places
For many causes

Now I have been
Waiting in the south balcony
To tell her the truth

And I am becoming
A piece of BLACK STONE
As the time runs apace!!

APRIL! APRIL!

You have come again
To me, you April
The Sky kisses the Earth
When she feels

My touch on her lip
Then it is evening
Then it is green grass
Then it is twinkling

In Her eyes some hope
Her lips are whispering
"What have you done?"
Her heart is singing

A song I have longed to hear
Since a pretty long time
"Have I done any wrong?"
I have no fear

Kalyan Chaudhury

Her silence is golden
Nature catches me
On my neck cloudy fingers
Show me two free

Birds in the open dark sky
Coming to their nest
Closing tired wings
Taking their rest

It has never happened
To the best of my knowledge
Only it is APRIL
It is a valued pledge!!

BOGTUI: 21.3.2022

One year ago
Can you remember
O Lady Kuro
What danger
Knocked at the door?

The friends of yours
Came at night
They were angels of course
Or medieval Knights

Took them to peace
Of Heaven
With the Fire-bliss
Still the raven

In the morning
Blames your friends
For that evening
For the flaming ends

Though nothing happened
On that day
People say
There comes your END!!

To the citizens of Troy

There comes the ship
Close your doors
The VOTE-WAVE roars
There reaches the Chief

Now the time is ripe
Tell the gatekeepers
Neither you are hers
Nor the news FIVE

The TROJAN horse
Is in the way
Keep away
From the hoax

Don't let the horse in
The city of TROY
It is a dark evening
The horse is not a toy

If the horse is inside
At the dead of night
The WOMB will be open
And the cheaters fight

To kill your sleep
Don't open the gate
The TROJAN horse
Is in the ship!!

The Crocodile and the Vagina

You sent your men
To RAPE us
They did it
Very nicely
How kind they were!
They took away
Our CLOTHINGS!
After many days
The CROCODILE
Sheds TEARS!
We are hiding ourselves
In the dark forest and hills
Waiting for their coming back
To us again
We, the VAGINAS
Will cut their PENISES
With our TEETH and CLAWS!!

Kalyan Chaudhury

Democracy????????.................

33 LIVES you have SNATCHED
STILL you are athirst for BLOOD
STILL you are hankering after POWER
STILL you wish NOBODY will go
Against your WILL
You will search every nook and corner

To catch THEM
Who DARE oppose YOU
"VOTERS are only NUMBERS
If they LIVE or DIE
Little it MATTERS

Because numbers are
AlWAYS NUMBERS

I am the QUEEN
Of all I survey

From the hills
To the BAY"
You snatched 33
33 become 3300000
And they are ALIVE
WAIT
BIRNAM FOREST is coming!!!

Flowers are no longer flowers
They have become VOLCANOES!!!!

Development

Development
Is on the move
Shut up
Development
Is on the move
Smoke is coming out
From the burnt bodies

Freedom from HUNGER
Freedom from CASTEISM
Freedom from RACEISM
Freedom from UNEMPLOYMENT

The BIRNAM FOREST IS NOT FAR BEHIND!!

Endless

Please tell her
I am at a loss
What to do
And where to cross!
Please tell her
I saw her in Summer Storm
When she was running
Forgetting everything
Like a white kite in the cloudy sky!
Please tell her
I knew her
When she was playing flute
In the flowers of the Spring
Melody was speaking her wish
Silently closing her eyes
As the Sun was setting
Behind our known Mango tree!!!

In memory of POTTAM HUNGI

Nobody killed you Pottam
It was a nonliving drone
That killed you
In the dark forest and hills

The forest, the hills, the creepers,
The grass and the soil whispered
In mournful numbers
"Our child is no more"

They ordered the flowers
Not to blossom
The birds not to sing
The butterflies not to fly

And they changed themselves
Into ANTIAIRCRAFT GUNS!!

Last Day of the Spring

Let not go the last day of the Spring
In vain
Let us go to the garden
To see the flowers of the morning

I will not tell you the words
You have already forgot
Lest you should be late
Lest you should be caught

In the fancy of the memory
Of the gone days
Listen cuckoos sing
Little squirrels are in hurry

Let us sit on the river bank
Only to thank
The wind that is blowing
In the last day of the Spring

Kalyan Chaudhury

Now may you go
Your boat is coming to take you
From this glory of lost Spring
In this painful morning!

Love

When the morning star
Is in the sky
When you get up
When the swallow comes
To the bed
When you pull my fingers
Round your neck
Small soft hair
Two cups of tea on the table
When comes the Sunshine
On the floor
When the door bell rings
I open the the door
Our son is back from office
When you kiss forehead
Of our daughter in law
When you say," Don't go now
Wait here a little!!!"

My Poem

What was kept in the glass
What was kept in the dish
What was kept in rice
What was kept in lips
What was kept on door
What was kept on floor
What was kept on old
Stain of iron string
What was kept on rings
Of golden wedding
What was kept in morning dream
Of the little costly sleep
What was kept in ears
Heard and unheard words
Sung and unsung songs
Done and undone mails
No colour on the nail
Of your ring finger
What was kept in
Fish and curry

What was kept in
Hustle and hurry
You and I didn't love
What was kept in tough
Rat race everyday
You and I always
From hills to bay
Said to eachother
We were alone
And we lived together!!!

Nobody knows

Nobody knows
How the girl was killed
At Kamduni
How the girl was killed
At Hanskhali
How Anis died
How women and a child
Were burnt in Bogtui
How Lalon Shekh died
Why rape of the woman
At Park Street
Was a small incident

Why MACBETH has murdered SLEEP!

PHOENIX

Our house was on FIRE
Who burnt our house?
It was you who did it
We put out the fire
And again we built it
Green grass, flowers, creepers,
Lizards, cats, dogs, cows,
Butterflies, birds and red ants
Helped us to do the same

We know
Again you will try
To burn our house

But GREEN GRASS and OTHERS
Are there ....

Kalyan Chaudhury

Please wait

Please wait my mud house

I'll go to your lap again

Sheuli flowers, I'll take you back in my Autumn

Baba said, "Don't hurt SHEULI flowers"

While collecting you very softly

The jack fruit tree, the mango tree, I'm coming

To you, please wait

Please wait my favourite false ceiling

I'll climb you up only to find the fairy Swords

And the historical Gun

Please wait 1970

Please wait my Youth

Please wait my Magic Realism

I'm coming back very soon!!!

In the Rainy Evening

Why have you come?

It is raining heavily

I have told you not to come

"I don't need a raincoat

to come to you"

Your answer

"You are incorrigibly a LOVER!"

"Don't talk now with mouth

Let us talk with our eyes"

Again you have become unknown to me!!!

Shut up

When I was ten
I wanted to say something
Parents said, "Shut up"
When I was fifteen
I wanted to say .....
"Shut up", said they
When I was twenty
I wanted to say .....
"Shut up", said my in - laws
When I was thirty
I wanted to say .....
"Shut up", my husband said
When I was fifty
I wanted to say .....
"Shut up", my children said
When I was sixty
I wanted to say ....
"Shut up", said DEATH!!!

Silence

Today I am Silent
But I can Speak
That you don't know
And you are violent!

The river is stopped flowing
By your dam barrage
One day it shall overflow
And break your courage!

The air is not blowing
Everyone is calm and cool
SPING THUNDER shall come
Wait, YOU FOOL!!

A dialogue: Spring and Monsoon

------ I am young and beautiful.
   Come to me handsome.

------ How can I go to you? I am very busy now.
   The fields are going to be pregnant with seeds.
   I have to go there for nice mating!

The young couples are athirst for LOVE - WATER.

Human beings, the animals, birds, insects, algae etc are
   calling me!

------ You poses to be the SAVIOUR of the Lust for
   Life! Then what is the use of my warm youth?
   I've just come from the Winter Palace frozen
   with ice!

Why are flowers on my body blooming? Why are the
   new leaves on the same desirous for orgasm?

------ Never we will meet Dearest! But if only storm is
pleased to listen to US, it is possible.

I'll unveil you and we're wondering to see each other in
an everlasting lustorous MATING!!!

The Autumn

The Autumn has come to see me

Sheuli flowers are raining over my head

Black beetles, millipedes, red ants, honeybees, mating
dogs etc

Are postering against us

"Live and let live!!!"

"The Earth is also ours!!!"

The humming bird is singing nicely the story of Lotus
and Lily

I can just pour the melody in my old flute!!!

The Birds

The migratory birds

Couldn't come down

Because of the SMOG

Just they were moving around

And around

At last being tired

They changed themselves

Into RAIN DROPS

And cleared the SMOG!!!

The Circus

Countrymen
Lend me your ears
The CLOWN
And the rattlle snakes

Are on the throne
Giving away prizes
To the hens
Which will lay eggs

For the snakes
And the CLOWN
Please lend me your ears
The eggs are falling down

Catch those now
Otherwise
Break the eggs
To be precise
Questions are vague

Neither trust the CLOWN
Nor the snakes
Eggs he bakes
And the snake is brown

TO SAVE THE EGGS
OR NOT TO Save
That is the question
Always wins the BRAVE!

Kalyan Chaudhury

The Dogs

The dogs eat
The dogs drink
The dogs sleep
The dogs like their chains
They discuss about these
Mine is Gold
Yours is Silver
Yours is Iron
Yours is Old

But ....

The Jungle - Lore

G. B. in the JUNGLE

Lion – the President
Tiger – the Secretary

Agendum – To protect Jungle – The Home Land

Honeybee says
"Homosapiens will burn our home at Mid Night"

All animals shout
"We must protect our MOTHER LAND"

Only Chameleons say
"Let us talk to the KILLERS"

All reject the proposal
Except the Donkeys

At Mid Night
The KILLERS come

But BRAVE HEARTS
Chase them away

From their MOTHER LAND!!!

To the Poets and Artists

You have a father

And a mother

Still you are

Licking the SLIPPERS!

Really you have

A father and a mother!

Do you know

What you have done?

You have made a drum

Out of your

DEAD MOTHER'S SKIN!

And you are beating the same

In the SLIPPERS ' name!!

Kalyan Chaudhury

The Sword of Democles

We sleep
Under the SWORD of DEMOCLES

Though convicted
We see the Beauty

It may be a CHILD

It may be a WOMAN

It may be a Man

It may be
A WATER HYACINTH!!

The Weather Cock

"Bombs kill children
Bullets kill men
The blind person can see"
Says the honey bee
The deaf and dumb persons
Have so many questions
They can speak with you
Disagrees only a few

Rats can catch cats
Balls hit bats
Read the writing on the wall
There will be a great fall

THERE IS A WEATHER COCK
Nobody ever spoke!

To MIRAJ, my friend

One month ago
I went to you
Then you were
Enjoying the view

Of the setting sun
I didn't say anything
But waited
The sun was setting

Stars came like fireflies
One after another
In the sky
I said, "My brother"

You looked back
And shouted
"You have come
My friend!"

I said, "Mosk calls
Go there right now"
"Your temple calls
Go and bow"

Miraj said so
Together we said
"We have no TEMPLE
And MOSK also"

Two friends
Embraced each other
Cried bitterly
After one year

Apart from Allah
Apart from Iswar
We were FRIENDS
Therefore

Together we work
Together we fight
For our cause
And for our Right!!

To My Children

What can I say
In this darkness?
Amidst madness
Can you cut hay?

When will the sun
Bring light to you?
Years after years
Only the same view

I have seen in the street
Love lies bleeding
What a morning
Night comes to greet!

Floods of happiness
Where are you?
Break the black
Change the hue

Fen of stagnant

Water will go

A new wave will show

A newborn vow

On the throne

Sits the child

Plays with sand

AND A CASTLE THEY BUILD!!

To the Killers

Let my TEARS blossom
As FLOWERS
Let my flowers change
Into BUDS

Let my buds
Go back to NATURE CELLS
Let my nature cells
Mingle with the STEM

Let my stem
Reach to the ROOTS
Let my roots
Call the WATER

Let my water
Call the RIVERS
Let my rivers
Go to the OCEAN

Now my ocean

Will give the CLARION CALL

To the TORNADO

To DESTROY

The PALACES of the SINNERS!!

To us

Few days ago
A girl
Was being stabbed
By a man
Before our eyes
We didn't help her
We didn't prevent him
Even we didn't shout
Even we didn't call the police
We passed by silently
And OUR COUNTRY
Lies BLEEDING!!!

My last love

Last day came my last love
"Why did you give me
The costly phone before going away?"
"I couldn't help but do it" is my reply
"Also I can't help but come to you
Again and again," she said drinking me
With her tearful eyes
"Please don't come here.
Your bright future
Is waiting for you.
Your handsome friend
Will be hurt if you don't love him."
"Please don't say so and hurt me.
My mother has told me not to come to you.
But she doesn't know you are the Old Man
And I am your Sea," she stooped to conquer!!!

My last love: 2

When you said, "Take bath"
I jumped into the ocean
When you said, "You need some warmth"
I ran into the volcano
When you said, "Stop"
I became a statue
You burst into tears,
"Come back Romeo, come my Love"
But I have been captive inside the Stone-Staue
From Time -Immemorial!!!

Nursery Rhyme

Twinkle twinkle
Little star
How I wonder
What you are

Robbing the poor
And pay the rich
Looters of BANKS
Are out of reach

L I C and others are
Taken by whom
GOLD and MONEY
Found in a room

TREASURE islands
Are in some hands
Most of the PEOPLE
Are beating bands

And calling the gods
Shouting at OTHERS
POVERTY they have suffered from
Also the forefathers!!

Nursery Rhyme: 2

Jack and Jill
Went up the HILL
To fetch some copper and iron
Aluminium indeed
They badly needed
But the villagers' protest went on

Jill and Jack
They were simple enough
To do good to them
And fulfill their claim
But the villagers only blamed

Jack and Jill
Who wanted to destroy the hill
For making a factory after
How innocently they were
Improving the villagers'

Lifestyle and area indeed
Industry they badly needed
School and Hospital
Standard International
But the villagers were
Stupid as usual

So Jack and Jill
Bombed on the hill

AND DEVELOPMENT will surely
Come there after!!

Nursery Rhyme: 3

Ba ba black sheep
Have you any wool?
Yes Sir yes Sir
Many bags full

One for N another for M
One for V another for Ni
Thousand crores for H
Thousand crores for Me

But Sir some problems
Are there in it
Economy will not
Always permit

I am economy
I am the King
I am the Night
I am Morning

I am the Sun
I am the Moon
I give you curse
I give you boon

One per cent people
Will have NINETY
Per cent treasure
That is Measure for Measure

But Sir the promises
You have given?
Then play the game
Of RELIGION!

I am the Monarch
Of all I survey
But Sir in vain

The STORM is postponed
It will rise AGAIN!!

Nursery Rhyme: 4

Aunty Aunty
Yes Voter
Eating Sarda
No my dear

Eating Narda
No my dear
Eating Schools
No my dear

Eating Colleges
No my dear
Eating municipalities
No my dear

Eating coal
No my dear
Eating stone
No my dear

Eating sand
No my dear
Cow trafficking
No my dear

Then what did you EAT?
During HUNGER STRIKE
Only I ate bread and Meat!!

To my Love

My Love, O my Love
Don't let me
Kiss you
Let me kiss the rain
Or I will miss you!
O Rain o my R
I want to drench with HER
In you
When will I have
Your view!
Please don't
Let me KISS YOU!!

To my Love: 2

Love O my Love
You came
To my house
To see your Ex
Wearing blue blouse!
Blue clouds came in
With you
As if they knew
You would Renew
The bird's eye view!

To you

Like a short story

Slowly I am finishing

Please don't pluck flowers

And make a garland

For me

But come to me

And love me

An unending STORY is on the MOVE!!

To You

DOGS are barking
SNAKES are crawling
That is THEIR nature
In the SKY is the VULTURE

Waiting for the MOMENT
Of your DEATH
FIGHT! FIGHT! don't GIVE UP
Till your LAST BREATH

Don't forget your PAST
How GLORIOUS it was
COWARDS die many times
PRITILATA but ONCE!!

English version of a Urdu poem "Fark sirf itna sa tha"

Four persons carried your palanquin

My cot was also carried by four

Flowers were showered on you

Those were also showered on me

The difference was you dressed yourself

And I was dressed by others!

You went to your house

I also went to my last resort

The difference was you could walk

And I was carried by others!

A function was held there

Here was also a function

The difference was people were laughing there

And people were crying here!

A priest was there

Here was also a priest

Hymns were chanted there

Here also those were chanted!

Fire was the witness there

Here fire burnt my body

The difference was people greeted you

And here people burnt me into ashes!!!

Who am I?

Before birth I was a zero

After death I'll be a zero

In between the two

I'm a poet, a painter, a reciter, a bohemian, a lover and
a fighter

I stood first

I stood last

I failed

I passed

I hate and I love

I cry and I laugh

I embrace my friend and stab him as well

I was stabbed by my friend and eventually I fell

On the road of the DEATH in the very afternoon

When YOU came to me like a GOLDEN BOON!!!

Kalyan Chaudhury

Who are they?

Kalpana Maity, Thakurmani Murmu, Shova Munda and
    Jayanti Singh Sardar
Are bunch of flowers!
Cluster of stars!
Wrath of Serfs!
Pieces of uncut diamonds!
Barrels of guns!
Flaming fields of LALGARH!
Agonies behind the bars
More than 10 years!!!

Why

When the sky was overcast
With clouds
You called the sun
When the sky was blue
You fired the sun
When darkness came
You sent fireflies to sing a song
When there was no friend
You sent a tree to me
I sat under its shadow
To save myself from the sun
"Now don't take this tree"
Whispered I
"I am your tree
I am your sun
I am your WELCOME
I am GOOD BYE!!!"

With an apology to GOLDING (the Nobel Laureate)

A woman is foolish
She demands EQUAL POWER
Of a MAN

She does not know
"She is greater than a man"

She gets a SPERM
She gives a BABY

She gets a ROOM
She makes it a HOME

"Who is my father?"
Says SATYAKAM

"No need to know this
I am JABALA

I am the MOTHER-COURAGE!!"
(dedicated to Neomi Campbell)

Yesterday, Today, Tomorrow

Why are your eyes full of tears?

Not at all tears

My poem

Why are you sweating?

Not at all sweating

Dew drops of morning

Your lips are bleeding

Not at all bleeding

The Sun is rising

Faces behind the bars

Agony in the ribcage!

Not at all agony

Flower show it is!

Red cactuses bloom in the Desert!!!

A Farce???

More than one hundred and fifty
Less than one lakh
I'm more than sixty
Gone through Pearl S Buck
Seen Ananda and Nunrul
In a pool of blood!
Next year blood makes a pool
9 women and 2 children Death-Clad!
Spring thunder gives a Clarion
Political power grows out
From the barrels of the GUN!!!

An imaginary conversation

.... What are you doing?

.... I'm trying to solve unemployment problem

.... But how?

.... I'm establishing a building

.... School?

.... No

.... College?

.... No

.... University?

.... Oh, no

.... Business-centre?

.... Yes

.... What business?

.... Religion -business!!!

An Ode to the People

One is Robber

Another one Thief

In the centre and state

Both are the Chief!

15 lakh to everyone

2 crore jobs per year

The Robber promised

Can you remember?

The Thief is a symbol of

Honesty from head to feet

But it is proved

The Thief is a cheat!

The Robber is a

James scam Bond

Don't vote him

Don't, Don't, Don't!

The Thief is a

Spider woman

Spreading her net

Captures stone and sand!

Not only those

Not only those

Selling occupation

From school to municipality

She is a conjunction!

Don't vote them

Don't vote them

In coming election

Your fate will be determined

By your selection!!!

Fall of Macbeth

.....Macbeth will be King but

killed by a person

not normally born ....Banquo's son the next

King

......Banquo, you've heard I'm immortal

......Yes my lord .They've also told the Birnam

Forest would come to you before death

......I fuck the witches! All are utter lies! I've

killed all opponents and burnt their houses!

Girls are raped! Nobody dares speak against

me! I am the Monarch of all I survey!

Let us return Banquo ....

.....My lord Banquo was killed but his son ran

away.

.....You stupid, you can't do anything perfectly.

Henceforth let make the life of the people

Hell

Where is the Birnam forest? Where is the

man not normally born?

(Gasping a soldier came) My lord Birnam forest

is coming!

......Destroy the forest immediately! ....

There is a fierce battle between Macbeth

and Macduff.

.......You can't defeat me! Ha, Ha, Ha!

........I'm Macduff.

I'm a cesarean baby!!!!

Govt. Sign-Board but.....

This road is maintained
By PWD
The bridge is inaugurated
By the honourable .....
The hospital is founded
By the honourable.....
The school is run
By the panchayat
All these are written
In the Govt. Sign-Board
But nothing exists
In reality
Please don't believe this
Anti propaganda
This is nothing but conspiracy
of the opponent
Caste your VOTE
For only DEVELOPMENT!!!

HOMO Sapiens

If I'm not homo sapiens

Who am I?

Love, Anger, Greed, Infatuation,

Power, Envy

Can't overpower me

I never escaped from the battle

But many times I escaped from jail

On seeing a rattle snake

I embraced the death

But they ran away

They feared to call spade a spade

TYRANT a Tyrant

Mere a school truant am I

Not homo sapiens

Claimed to be honest

To speak the truth

I lit a fire in the dry leaves

In many villages

I touched the fire in the veins

Of Girls and Boys

Stream of blood from North to South

From East to West

Heaps of bones like the Himalayas

I've carried on my back

I'm one of the sons of the stupid Old Man

Taking birth many times

Defying Death many times

Cleaning the Earth many times!!!

HUNGER and FOOD

Few bags of "broken stars"

Had fallen last night

On the road

There was a grand feast

In the village

"Broken stars" were roasted

And served among the villagers

They ate them to their heart's content

And happily went to sleep

Dreaming when the other stars

Would be changed into RICE

And the sun and the moon

Would be nicely cooked

For their lunch and dinner

Because VOTE is coming

Because they are the VOTERS

Kalyan Chaudhury

Because came the leaders

With their cadres

With their golden promises

To fill their hungry stomachs

With delicious dishes

Still they are sleeping

Eating "broken stars"

VOTE is coming

And they are the VOTERS!!!

I Can

I can hear
Dry leaves falling
Little twigs whirling
Volcanoes breathing!

Kalyan Chaudhury

If you.....

If you can't read
Read my poems
If you can't write
Read my poems
If you can't eat
Read my poems
If you can't breathe
Read my poems
If you can't love
Read my poems
If you can't live
Read my poems!!!

Last love: 3

--- You'll not get what you want.

   Again you've come to me.

---Yes, I know.

   Still I come to you.

---Then why have you come?

---I've come to see your eyes.

   If you wish you

may talk to me.

   If you don't I'll say nothing.

---You are too foolish to love me.

--- I don't want to be smart to get you.

---You FOOL, hug me right now!

The glow-worms become stars then and there!!!

Love

When the sun rises
When the sun sets
When the moon rises
When the moon sets
When the stars twinkle
When the wind blows
When the sky is blue
When the sky is overcast
When comes the storm
When comes the rain
When the naked tree
Is in full bloom
When Tagore's song is sung
By George Biswas
"Thine is this a beginning
Mine is also the ending......."
When writes Thomas Man
The unique "Black Swan"
When Ramkinkar and his Radha
Become necessity of ART

When Jean Paul Sartre
And Simone de Beauvoir
Kiss each other
When Surya Sen leaves
His newly married WIFE
For ever
LOVE says, "Thou hast made me endless
Such is thy pleasure!!!"

Man is Mortal

.....I'm getting a smell

.....I'm also getting a smell

.....Something is burning

.....History, Geography, Science

.....Biology, Geology, Evolution

.....You better call EL NINO

.....But don't forget ELECTION

.....Gods in the DOLLS 'HOUSE'

.....Save cows, Swines for export

.....Don't forget to drink COW 'SURINE'

.....Forget HUNGER INDEX, UNEMPLOYMENT

.....SYCOPHANTS of the BRITISH IMPERIALISM

      Should be our PATHFINDERS

.....Burn the minorities to make tea

.....SPRING THUNDER when will you come

      AND MAKE US FREE, MAKE US FREE????

New Nursery Rhyme: 1

Food, shelter, clothing
Nothing Nothing Nothing
Robbery and setting
Both are existing!
Theft and cheating
Forget your eating
Shelter and clothing
All for VOTING!
Health and Education
Go to damnation
Pray to "RUM" for
Only ELECTION!
Twinkle Twinkle
Little star
Forget Food Clothing
And Shelter!!!

New Nursery Rhyme: 2

Ba Ba Black sheep

Have you looted treasure?

Yes voter, yes voter

Food, clothing, shelter!

One percent has had

Seventy percent of yours

Coal, gold, sand,

Cow-Trafficking, ores!

SARDA, NARDA and

School service commission

Ration of the people,

Municipal corporation!

We are leaders

We are looters

We are V M and N M

Few of the robbers!

Ba ba black sheep

Have you any wool?

Yes VOTER, you are

Nothing but FOOL!!!

New Nursery Rhyme: 3

....Tea seller! Tea seller!

....Yes customer

....Two crore jobs per year?

....I don't know where

....Rs fifteen lakh to all?

....I don't know at all

....Black money recovery?

....Why are you in hurry?

....Looting of banks

By your friends?

....Don't you know

The modern trends?

....Then you are a FRAUD

....Ha! Ha! Ha!

New Nursery Rhyme: 4

A robber became the King
A thief the Queen
The robber started looting
The thief was following!
His friends took loans
From the banks
And ran away
To the foreign lands!
The robber said to
All and sundry
"Please don't
Be angry!"
"Each will get fifteen lakh
And two crore jobs per year
The whole black money
Soon I recover!"
But ten years gone
No promises were kept
People rushed to the King
But he slept and slept!!!

New Nursery Rhyme: 5

"Queen Aunty, Queen Aunty
Where have you been?"
"I have been to many places
Only for eating!"
"Please tell me, please tell me
What you have eaten"
"Coal, gold, sand, stone
And Cow-Trafficking!
School service commission
And municipal
Corporation alongwith ration
Of beloved people!
I've forgot to mention
SARDA and NARDA case
Eating these in few years
Is really a hard task!!!"

New Nursery Rhyme: 6

"King uncle, King uncle
Where have you been?"
"I've been to many places
Only for cheating!"
"Please tell me, please tell me
What you've cheated"
"Many promises I didn't keep
But still people greeted!
Two crore jobs per year
And fifteen lakh to all
I promised but now
Not at all, not at all!
Not only that before voting
I raised my voice
'I'll defeat enemies
That is my choice!'
So Pulwama happened
So Rumlala fest
Before voting, before voting
I've done my best!!!"

New Nursery Rhyme: 7

King and Queen
Started to reign
To cheat the people
Again and again!
King wanted power
By hook or crook
Queen did the same
What shook
The daily life of people!
They didn't bother the sufferings
They caused to men, women
And helpless cattle!
Houses were on fire
Godhra It might be
It might be Bogtui
So shameless He and SHE!!!

One day in the Book Fair

....Good morning Sir,

You are a great leader!

....Thanks

....What are you eating?

....Mutton Biriyani

....Have you bought any book?

....Oh no!

....Why sir?

....If you go to zoo will you purchase any animal?

Prayer of Winter

O Sun my dearest Sun

Where are you?

The sky is cloudy

Footpath is soaked with dew

We are shivering with cold

And hunger

So sad we are

And our Mother

Is waiting for your light

Our father has been missing

Long ago

In a street-fight

O Sun our dearest Sun

We can't bear this

DARKNESS! DARKNESS!

Give me your KISS

Please send the Spring

Please send our Father

Again he'll sing

And call our MOTHER!!!

Kalyan Chaudhury

Problems and Solutions

....Food?

....Rumlala

....Clothing?

....Rumlala

....Shelter?

....Rumlala

....Health?

....Rumlala

....Education?

....Rumlala

....Intellectuals with SPINES?

....Vima Koregaon Case!!!

Tell Me

Tell me where
Land is snatched
From farmers
Salt water enters
Into their fields
To grow fishes
That is a great deal!
Tell me where
Housewives are
Summoned at night
By the leader
But they have no right
To stop predator
Only their tears
Become nightmares!!!

The Boy and His Mother (land)

....Why are you going

     To the King's palace at night?

....The King calls me

....Why don't you refuse to go?

...I'm afraid of the King

...Already he looted your land

     Why don't you use arrow and bow?

....I'm worried about your safety

...No mom that can't be

     Dress me like a soldier

     Give me the sword of my father

....Don't go my son .Remember

     Your father's failure

....Now people are with me

     Surely we'll snatch the VICTORY!!!

The Handkerchief

.....Where is my handkerchief?

.....I don't know my lord

.....Don't tell a lie .It is with Iago.

.....I don't know how he got it

.....You traitor.Now pray to God before death.

.....Don't kill me.My only sin that I love you.

.....Be ready for death

.....Don't kill her.She is innocent.

.....Who are you? Don't disturb me.

.....I'm the Handkerchief running here to save Desdemona

.....You are a liar

.....My lord, then call Iago at once

.....Okay I'll send a soldier to call the bustard

.....Desdemona,my love come to me .Please forgive me.

My love,my minutes are numbered. I've taken poison. I've been always faithful to you. Good Bye!!!

The Kiss

— Did you forsake me?

— Not at all

— Then why did you say," My days are

　　numbered?"

— Because you ignored me

— Why didn't you allow me to touch you?

— Because you were scared lest enemies should

know our LOVE

— Okay I won't be scared

The lover's lane readily changed into G T Road

The winter into SPRING

The pond into OCEAN

Two bodies into ONE!!!

To the PIG-STY Goers

Who are you pigsty goers?
Did you drink mother's milk?
Did you love your kith and kin?
Are you free from casteism?
Aren't you a band of goondas?
Didn't you spread your empire
Throughout the COUNTRY?

Then what is the use of any
Mega manifestation of ELECTION???

To the Capitalism

Orbits of the Solar System, Stars
And other heavenly bodies
Are satellites to you
Very soon you'll sell them
To the Tycoons
Already you've eaten the lungs of the Earth
No longer you are Homo Sapiens
As you are drinking blood and sweat of Human
Beings
Red Ants are crossing deserts, mountains and
Oceans
The storm is only postponed
The STORM will rise again!!!